# LITTLE
# GREY RABBIT'S
# COUNTRY
# BOOK

## GAIL DUFF

Illustrated by Margaret Tempest
and Valerie Greeley

COLLINS

William Collins Sons & Co Ltd
London · Glasgow · Sydney · Auckland
Toronto · Johannesburg

The Margaret Tempest illustrations in this book
have been taken from
Little Grey Rabbit's Valentine
Little Grey Rabbit's Pancake Day
Hare and the Easter Eggs
Wise Owl's Story
Little Grey Rabbit's Washing Day
Little Grey Rabbit's Birthday
Grey Rabbit's May Day
Grey Rabbit and the Circus
The Knot Squirrel Tied
Little Grey Rabbit and the Weasels
Little Grey Rabbit Makes Lace
Little Grey Rabbit's Party
Fuzzypeg Goes to School
Hare and Guy Fawkes
Little Grey Rabbit Goes to the Sea
The Speckledy Hen
Moldy Warp the Mole
Squirrel Goes Skating
Little Grey Rabbit's Christmas

All illustrations other than by Margaret Tempest are by
VALERIE GREELEY
Book design by Enid Fairhead FCSD

FOR LUCY

First published 1990
A CIP catalogue record for this book is available from the British Library.
ISBN 0 00 194293-X

Printed and bound in Great Britain
by William Collins & Co Ltd, Glasgow

# CONTENTS

# INTRODUCTION

Little Grey Rabbit, Squirrel and Hare lived together in a small house in the country. They were comfortable and very happy, although they had none of the things that we are used to today, such as electricity, or television, or running water. Like many country people before them, they knew how to do without these things. They made their own candles and lights, heated their oven with a wood fire, sang songs and told stories to each other to keep themselves amused and carried water in buckets from the stream.

Grey Rabbit went to the market for food, but she, Hare and Squirrel grew many of their own vegetables and knew which wild plants, nuts and berries were good to eat.

If Hare wanted anything really special, such as fireworks or chocolate Easter eggs, he bravely went to the village shop and his friend the cat helped him to get them. Usually, though, all presents were made by the animals themselves from things they could find in the countryside, such as nut shells, sheep's wool and feathers. Fuzzypeg found his toys in the countryside, smooth stones to play five-stones and oak-apples to use as marbles.

There were no chemist's shops or doctors, but Grey Rabbit knew just which herbs would cure the coughs and colds and other small things the animals had wrong with them.

In the country, changing seasons are noticed and the animals had different things to do in spring, summer, autumn and winter. They did the garden in spring, had picnics in the hayfields in summer and bonfires in the autumn and celebrated Christmas with carols and mince-pies and presents round the tree.

We are lucky. We have warm houses, lights that come on when you flick a switch and shops full of everything that we need. We can enjoy all these, and we can enjoy the things that Grey Rabbit enjoyed too.

We can remember all the special days in the year like St Valentine's Day, Easter, May Day, Midsummer, Bonfire Night and Christmas. We can have parties and processions, make special foods and send home-made cards and gifts.

We can take a walk in the country or the park and find flowers and seeds, nuts and berries for pressing or using to make toys. We can make our own lights and candles and sew patchwork.

We can play all the old party games and, instead of watching television, sit round together to tell stories and sing songs.

So, whether you live in the country or the town, get ready to enjoy some of the best things in Little Grey Rabbit's year.

# SPRING

There is excitement in the air in spring. It is the beginning of a new season, the days are getting longer and warmer and the sun begins to get up earlier, shining in Grey Rabbit's window, reminding her that there are a lot of things to do. She must get out her brooms and dusters ready for spring cleaning and send Hare and Squirrel out into the garden to start growing vegetables.

There are Valentine cards to make, pancakes to mix and Easter eggs to decorate and the first herbs and flowers to be found in the hedgerows.

## ST VALENTINE'S DAY

*St Valentine's Day. St Valentine's Day.*
*The birds are courting and kissing today.*
*We love one another whatever you say.*
*We are all very happy this Valentine's Day.*

St Valentine's Day is on February 14th and, on the day before, Grey Rabbit, Squirrel, Hare and the other woodland animals were very busy, making cards and wrapping presents to give to their friends and loved ones.

### Valentine cards

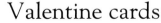

The first Valentine cards were often decorated with pictures of flowers and hearts or were cut out in a heart shape with a lace edging. Grey Rabbit, Squirrel and Hare made their own Valentine cards and it is fun to do the same.

The person who sends a Valentine card should never write their name on it for, as Grey Rabbit told Squirrel and Hare, "It is a surprise. You try to guess."

DEAR GREY RABBIT

# Make Grey Rabbit's Valentine card

Grey Rabbit's Valentine card had on it a picture of a heart, painted with tiny flowers round the edge, and *'Dear Grey Rabbit'* written on it.

To make this card, you will need:

1 piece thin white card 33cm × 18cm (13 in × 7 in)
1 piece paper (any sort, even newspaper) 16.5cm × 18cm
(6½ in × 7 in)
pencil
scissors
coloured pencils, paints or felt tipped pens

Fold the card in half to give you a Valentine card that will measure 16.5cm (6½ in) across and 18cm (7 in) down.

If you are good at drawing you may lightly pencil in the shape of a large heart directly onto the card. If you would rather have a guide, make a template from the piece of paper.

Fold the paper in half from top to bottom. Your folded edge should measure 18cm (7 in).

On one side of the paper, draw half a heart against the fold. Cut out the heart shape. Open out the paper.

Lay the paper over the front of the card and lightly draw round the cut-out shape. This pencilled-in heart should not show when the card is finished, so do not press too hard.

Draw flowers, about 2.5cm (1 in) across around the heart. Colour them in. Or you can make tissue paper flowers and stick them round the heart. Write a message in the centre of the heart such as 'With love' or 'For you on Valentine's Day'.

If you can, think up a rhyme for the inside.

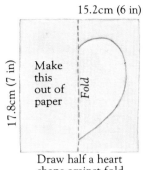

15.2cm (6 in)

17.8cm (7 in)

Make this out of paper

Fold

Draw half a heart shape against fold

Cut out paper template

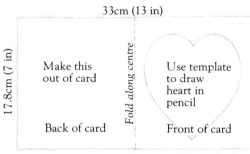

33cm (13 in)

17.8cm (7 in)

Make this out of card

Back of card

Fold along centre

Use template to draw heart in pencil

Front of card

16.5cm (6½ in)

Draw flowers around heart

*With Love*

Long before people gave presents at Christmas it was the custom to give presents as tokens of love on St Valentine's Day.

Suitable small Valentine presents to give with your card can include handkerchiefs, little bags of pot pourri, bookmarks, tiny ornaments or packets of sweets. Hide your presents round the house as Grey Rabbit did. If you cannot think of a rhyme to give as a clue simply write 'Look under the chair' or wherever you have decided to hide your present. Put a decorated label on the present that reads 'With love'.

To scent your card, put a small drop of perfume onto a piece of cotton wool. Do not make it wet, one drop is enough. Rub the cotton wool over the card.

# PANCAKE DAY

Pancake Day falls on a Tuesday, about six weeks before Easter. A long time ago, people had to give up eating meat, eggs and milk for Lent and on Pancake Day the last of the milk and eggs had to be used up.

In some villages, pancake bells were rung early in the morning and again in the evening and between this time you could cook and eat as many pancakes as you liked. In the village near Grey Rabbit's house the church bells rang at midday to signal that pancake making could begin.

## How to make pancakes

Pancakes are easy to mix and to cook, but it is best to let a grown-up help you with the stove and the hot pan.

You will need:

large mixing bowl
large wooden spoon
frying pan
fish slice
small pan to melt the butter in

INGREDIENTS FOR 8 PANCAKES

100g (4 oz) wholemeal flour
pinch salt
1 egg
1 egg yolk
150ml ($\frac{1}{4}$ pint) milk mixed with 150ml ($\frac{1}{4}$ pint) water
15g ($\frac{1}{2}$ oz) butter, melted
small knob of butter or $\frac{1}{2}$ tablespoon vegetable oil for frying each pancake

Put the flour and salt into a mixing bowl. Make a well in the centre of the flour. Put the egg and egg yolk into the well. Using the wooden spoon, begin to beat in flour from the sides of the well. Pour in a little of the milk and water mixture and beat it well. Continue doing this until you have used up half the milk and water mixture. Beat in the melted butter and then the rest of the milk and water. Beat well until you see bubbles come on the surface of the batter. Leave the batter in a cool place for 30 minutes.

When you are ready to cook the pancakes, give the batter another stir. Heat some butter or oil in your frying pan on a medium heat. Put in 2 tablespoons of the batter and quickly tip it around so that it spreads out thinly and has a lacy edge. Peep under one side of your pancake with the fish slice. If the underside is golden brown, turn the pancake over. You can either do this with the fish slice or, of you are feeling brave, you can toss it.

Tossing a pancake is actually quite easy. Take the handle of the frying pan in both hands. Use oven gloves if it is hot. Shake the pancake to make sure it will not stick to the pan. Now flip the pan upwards, bringing the outer edge slightly towards you. The pancake should be lifted only a little way into the air and should flip over as it starts to come down. If you have been successful, brown the other side of the pancake.

When both sides are done, slide the pancake onto a warm plate. If no one minds your making a mess in the kitchen, you could try what Grey Rabbit and her friends did. Toss the pancake high in the air and let everyone try to catch it on their plates. Whoever catches it can eat it. But be fair. Make sure that everyone gets one.

Traditionally, pancakes are flavoured with a squeeze of lemon juice and sprinkling of sugar or spoonful of melted honey. Roll them up and eat with a spoon and fork.

Pancakes can also make savoury meals. Vegetables in a cheese sauce or a savoury minced beef make good fillings.

## FLAVOURING THE BATTER

Both Grey Rabbit and Moldy Warp flavoured their batter with herbs. Grey Rabbit added the juice of wild wood sorrel leaves to hers. You can have the same effect by adding the grated rind of a lemon or orange before the batter is cooked.

Moldy Warp sweetened his batter with honey and added wild thyme for flavour. If you wish, you can add 1 tablespoon sugar or honey to your batter to make a sweet pancake.

A pinch of mixed herbs added to the batter gives a good flavour to pancakes that are going to have a savoury filling.

# Having a pancake party

Why not ask your friends to come and enjoy Pancake Day with you? Perhaps each person could provide a separate ingredient. One could bring the flour, another the butter and so on. Mix up several bowls full of batter and all take turns to add the eggs, or beat or add the milk.

After you have eaten the pancakes, you can all sing Grey Rabbit's Pancake Day Song.

*Pancake Day! Pancake Day!*
*Fuzzy and Mole have come to play.*
*Grey Rabbit will toss it*
*And Hare will eat it.*
*And Squirrel will catch it on Pancake Day.*

*Pancake Day! Pancake Day!*
*A pancake for Squirrel,*
*A pancake for Mole,*
*A snippet for Rabbit*
*Down in a hole,*
*A piece for Owl*
*Up in the tree,*
*And a very small pancake for Fuzpeg and me.*

# EASTER

Everyone is happy at Easter time for they know that spring is really here and that most of the bad weather is past. Spring flowers decorate our gardens and the countryside and the farmers' crops begin to grow. A spring chicken coming out of an egg is a sign of all this new life and so we eat eggs at Easter, decorate them and give them as presents.

The animals believed that the sun danced for joy on Easter morning. They got up early to watch it and to hear the birds singing their Easter hymn.

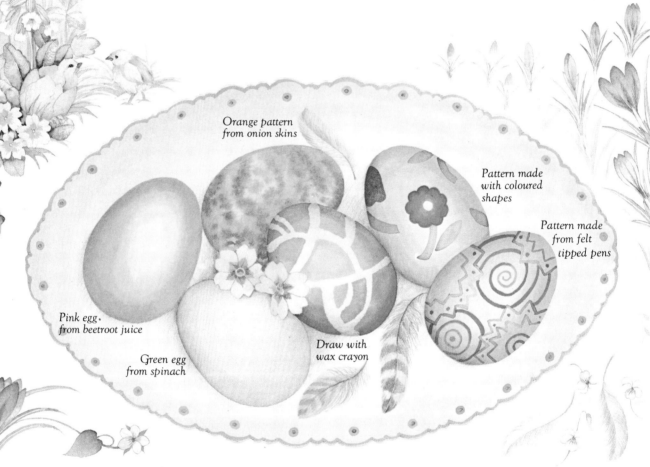

*Orange pattern from onion skins*

*Pattern made with coloured shapes*

*Pattern made from felt tipped pens*

*Pink egg from beetroot juice*

*Green egg from spinach*

*Draw with wax crayon*

## Decorating eggs for Easter

You can decorate real eggs and either eat them for breakfast on Easter morning, take them on an Easter picnic, use them in Easter games, or simply have them as an Easter decoration.

To colour eggs, boil them in water to which you have added 1 tablespoon vinegar and a few drops of food colouring.

If you would rather use a home-made dye, you can use the water that spinach was boiled in to colour the eggs green or beetroot water for pink.

To make a pattern on your eggs, draw it before boiling them in the coloured water, using either a white crayon or a small white candle.

You will get a pretty orange pattern on the shell if you wrap your eggs in onion skins before boiling them. Keep the skins on with a rubber band.

For hard boiled eggs, you will need to cook them for 10-12 minutes. Cool them completely. Eggs boiled without colouring can be decorated with coloured pencils, felt-tipped pens or paints. You can also stick on gummed paper shapes.

14

# Easter egg games

These games were once played all over Britain at Easter time.

EGG ROLLING
Roll your eggs down a steep hill. The winner is not the one whose egg gets to the bottom first, but the one whose egg goes furthest without cracking or breaking.

EGG SHACKLING
Shake the eggs in a bag or blanket. The winner is the one whose egg lasts the longest.

EGG TOSSING
Throw your egg from hand to hand. Again, the winner is the owner of the egg that does not break.

EGG TAPPING
Two people tap their eggs together. The one whose egg breaks first has to pay a forfeit.

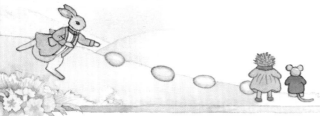

# Make your own Easter eggs

Eggs made with ground almonds and with a gooey yellow centre are easier to make than chocolate eggs.

For 10 eggs, you will need:
175g (6 oz) ground almonds
100g (4 oz) honey
225g (8 oz) icing sugar
1 egg white
yellow food colouring
chocolate vermicelli

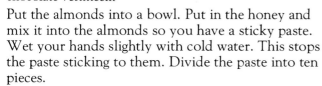

Put the almonds into a bowl. Put in the honey and mix it into the almonds so you have a sticky paste. Wet your hands slightly with cold water. This stops the paste sticking to them. Divide the paste into ten pieces.

Put the icing sugar into another bowl. Beat the egg white so it begins to get frothy. Add it to the icing sugar together with a few drops of yellow food colouring. Mix well with a spoon to an even, gooey mixture. Divide it into ten pieces.

Take a piece of the almond paste and flatten it slightly in the palm of your hand. Put a portion of the icing sugar mixture on top. Carefully mould the paste round the icing sugar so it covers it all round. Make the paste into an egg shape. Roll the 'egg' in the chocolate vermicelli. Do the same with the other pieces of paste and icing sugar. When all the eggs are done, wrap them separately in clingfilm.

# Easter presents

Both Squirrel and Rat made eggs that you could not eat but which contained presents for Grey Rabbit. You can buy cardboard eggs, both small and large, and put Easter presents inside. Sweets, fluffy chicks, small toys, necklaces or bracelets, handkerchiefs or small ornaments are all suitable things, or anything else that is small and that you can easily buy with your pocket money.

# SPRING CLEANING

When the spring sun shines in through the windows it shows up all the dust that has collected in dark corners of the house during the winter. It is time to get out the brushes and brooms and make the house spic-and-span for the summer.

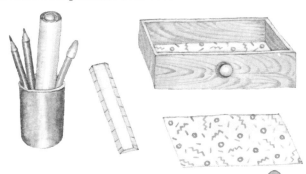

How about cleaning out your toy cupboard or book shelves? You will probably be surprised at how untidy and dusty they have become. First take everything out of the cupboard or off the shelves. Sort out all the things. There will be a lot that you will want to keep. Some that are too young for you can be given away to younger brothers or sisters or to friends. There will probably be some things that are not worth keeping, such as broken crayons or old boxes or cardboard tubes that you thought might one day be useful. Be brave and throw these away. Give everything that you want to keep a rub with a duster or a damp cloth.

Next, wipe over the shelves with a damp cloth. Grey Rabbit lined Wise Owl's shelves with beech leaves. Ask the grown-ups in your family if they have a left-over roll of wallpaper or sticky backed plastic for your shelves. Keep the wallpaper in place with drawing pins.

Now put back tidily all the things that you have decided to keep, and you have finished your spring cleaning.

## Make a polishing duster

You will need:

125ml (4fl oz) linseed oil (you can buy this in an ironmonger's)
125ml (4fl oz) malt vinegar
an old plate
a clean duster

Measure out the oil and vinegar and pour them into a jar with a screw-top lid. Screw the lid on tightly. Shake the jar well to mix the oil and vinegar. Pour a little of the mixture onto an old plate. Press the duster onto the mixture so that it soaks into it. You will now have a cloth that polishes as it dusts.

## Make drawer liners

You will need:

white wallpaper lining paper or a plain coloured wallpaper
ruler
scissors
crayons or felt tipped pens

Measure the inside of your drawer. Cut out a piece of paper that fits exactly inside. With crayons or felt tipped pens, draw a pattern or picture on the paper. Put it into your drawer.

## Washing

Spring is also a time for washing all the thick winter clothes and putting them away until they are needed again next year.

Why not try washing some of your own clothes? Choose a fine sunny day, and take them into the garden to wash them.

You will need two plastic washing bowls. Fill one with warm water and another with cold water. Stir soap powder into the warm water and leave the cold water as it is.

One at a time, put your clothes into the soapy water. Squeeze them and then give them a good rub. Squeeze out as much water as you can, and put the clothes into the bowl of plain cold water. When all the clothes are in the cold water, throw the soapy water away but keep the empty bowl near you.

Dunk each garment up and down separately and then squeeze as much water from it as you can. Put it into the empty bowl.

Before Grey Rabbit bought her clothes pegs from the Gypsy Rabbit, she hung her washing on the bushes around her garden. You can do this if the day is not too windy.

## Make lavender water

for rinsing your clothes

You can make your clothes smell sweet and fresh if you add lavender water to the rinse. To make it, put 4 tablespoons of dried lavender flowers into a saucepan with 850ml ($1\frac{1}{2}$ pints) of cold water. Get a grown-up to put the saucepan on the stove for you and bring the water to the boil. Turn down the heat and put a lid on the pan. Let the water simmer gently for 30 minutes. Take the pan off the heat and let the water cool down. Strain the water. Add the lavender water to the rinsing water before you put in your clothes. When your clothes are dry, fold them neatly and put them away. You can make a scented drawer liner to keep them smelling sweet.

## Make a scented drawer liner

You will need:

A drawer liner made as opposite
small piece of cotton wool
perfume or toilet water
large polythene bag
elastic band

Spread out your drawer liner. Put about four drops of perfume or toilet water on the cotton wool. Rub it all over the drawer liner (on the back, if you have used felt tipped pens). Roll up the drawer liner. Put it into the polythene bag with the cotton wool. Secure the top of the bag with an elastic band. Leave the liner for 1 week. Then put it into your drawer.

# FLOWERS, PLANTS and TREES
## to look for in spring

If you go for a walk in the country or even in the park in the spring, look out to see how many wild flowers and plants that you can find.

Here are some that Grey Rabbit would have found in the fields and woods near her house.

## Hazel catkins

Squirrel picked two clusters of hazel catkins to give to the gypsy so she could use them as ear-rings. You will find hazel trees along hedgerows, on scrub land and in some woods. Pick the catkins in clusters of two or more and hang them over your ears so that they dangle down.

## Pussy willows

The catkins of some willow trees, that you will find growing near streams and ponds, are short and fluffy. They look rather like fluffy kittens and they are called pussy-willows.

To make a *cat picture* with pussy willows and hazel catkins you will need a piece of thick paper and some glue.

Break off the fluffy catkins from the pussy-willow stalks. Stick them onto the paper. Stick on hazel catkins to make tails. If the dark brown, pointed parts of the outer casing of the pussy-willows are still on the stalks, stick these on to make ears.

Make a whole family of cats and kittens on the paper and draw a spring picture round them.

## NETTLES

In the spring, the soft tops of young stinging nettles can be used to make soup. Wear gloves to pick them, but the sting will disappear as soon as the nettles are cooked.

## DANDELIONS

Add a few chopped young dandelion leaves to salads and sandwiches. Hare used a dandelion's seed head to tell the time. Blow the seed head, or dandelion clock, to find out what time it is. If you need four blows it is four o'clock, if six blows it is six o'clock, time for supper!

## WOOD SORREL

This delicate little plant grows in woods and shady places. Its leaves are divided into three parts. Grey Rabbit put the leaves into salads and squeezed the juice into her pancakes.

## COLTSFOOT

Coltsfoot is one of the first flowers to appear in the spring. It has fluffy yellow flowers, each on a single, thick stem. There are purple coloured scales on the stem and the leaves are large and hoof-shaped. Coltsfoot grows mainly on waste ground.

Grey Rabbit would have kept coltsfoot syrup in her medicine cupboard. This is how she would have made it.

50g (2 oz) coltsfoot stems
150ml ($\frac{1}{4}$ pint) water
350g (12 oz) dark brown sugar

Cut the stems into pieces about 2.5cm (1 in) long. Put them into a saucepan with the water and sugar. Put the saucepan on a low heat and stir with a wooden spoon until the sugar dissolves. Let the syrup come to the boil. Get a grown-up to help you skim off any scum which comes to the top. Boil the syrup for 30 minutes.

Line a sieve with muslin or a clean, washed-out tea towel. Pour the syrup through it into a bowl. Pour the warm syrup into jars.

When you have a cough, you can either eat a spoonful straight from the jar, or dilute it with hot water to make a soothing drink.

## PRIMROSES

Grey Rabbit used to make wine from primrose flowers, but there are not enough primroses in the countryside now for us to be able to pick them. Walk along country lanes and beside hedges to see how many you can spot.

## VIOLETS

Grey Rabbit loved violets because they are so pretty and they smell so sweet. The flowers of violets can be candied to make cake decorations.

# PLANTING A GARDEN

Hare, Squirrel and Grey Rabbit grew their own vegetables and always had flowers in their garden.

Before you plant anything, you will need to get the soil ready. Dig it over first and then rake it to make the top soil fine. Large lumps will squash the seedlings. Do not sow seeds if the soil is too wet or too dry. It is best if it is just a little bit damp.

If your garden is small, or you do not have a garden at all, you can grow both vegetables and flowers in tubs, large plant pots or window boxes. Make sure there are holes in the bottom for water to drain through and put a layer of broken clay pots or stones in the bottom. Fill your container with potting compost. You will have to buy this from a shop or a garden centre. Ask the shopkeeper to tell you which is the best type.

## Growing vegetables

Vegetables are best grown in rows. This makes weeding easy and also lets you fit more into your garden plot.

Sow seeds in a straight row; gardeners use a long line of string which is wound half on one stick and half on another. One stick is stuck into the ground at one end of the row. String is unwound from the second stick, which is then stuck into the ground to mark the other end of the row.

Using a narrow stick, draw it along the string so that it makes a shallow trench in the ground. Tear the top off your seed packet and pour about 1 teaspoon of the seeds into your hand. Thinly sprinkle them along your trench. Put back any you have left in your hand. Using the back of a rake, push the soil back over the seeds. Firm it down by gently tapping along the row with the upright rake. If you are growing seeds in tubs or boxes, sprinkle them thinly over the top of the compost and cover them with a fine sprinkling of soil or more compost.

## Taking care of your seeds

Water your seeds every day if the weather is dry. Use a watering can fitted with a sprinkler. If you pour water out with no sprinkler, the seeds will get washed away.

Grey Rabbit knew that the wind sows dandelion seeds. It can also sow other weed seeds that we do not want on the vegetable patch, so you must weed your plot often. Wait until your vegetables have come up, so that you can see exactly where they are and where the weeds are.

# Some vegetables to grow

### LETTUCES

Once the lettuce plants are about 7.5cm (3 in) high, they need to be thinned out. This means that some must be pulled out to leave you with a gap of about 15cm (6 in) between the plants that are left. You can eat the leaves of the plants you pull out.

### RADISHES

These grow quickly but they all need to be picked at once. Sow only a short row at a time.

### SPRING ONIONS

These do not need thinning out.

### CARROTS

These must be thinned out, too. Leave a gap of about 2.5cm (1 in) between each plant. If possible, take out the smaller seedlings, leaving the larger ones to grow.

# Some flowers to grow

### SUNFLOWERS

These grow very tall so put them at the back of your plot. As each sunflower grows it will need to be tied to a long pole to stop it from falling over.

### NASTURTIUMS

Buy a packet that gives you both yellow and orange flowers. These will grow anywhere.

### STOCKS

These smell lovely. Grow them like Love-in-a-mist.

### SWEET PEAS

Grow them at the back of your plot and provide them with a net or trellis to climb up.

### MARIGOLDS

Buy mixed packets so you get different colours of yellow and orange. The seeds are large and easy to spread out thinly.

### LOVE-IN-A-MIST

These are small blue flowers which look rather like pom-poms in the middle of a lot of feathery leaves. To plant them, smooth over a small patch of soil, scatter the seeds over it and cover them up with a thin layer of more soil.

# SUMMER

Summer is a time for doing things and finding things out of doors. Grey Rabbit, Squirrel and Hare began the summer with a May Day procession and, in the fine sunny days, watched a circus, went haymaking and enjoyed eating the food from their garden out of doors. You can do the same.

You can also look for wild flowers and garden flowers and use the most common ones for summer crafts.

It was Grey Rabbit's birthday on Midsummer Day, so celebrate it with a picnic.

## MAY DAY

For many hundreds of years, May Day has been celebrated as the first day of summer. There were once processions through the streets led by a King and Queen of the May. Everyone carried garlands of flowers and there was music, Morris dancing and, later, dancing round the May-pole. Go out early on May Day morning, scoop some dew from the grass and rub it on your face. It is said to make you beautiful and keep you young. Grey Rabbit gave some to old Miss Susan to make her feel young again.

# May garlands

The children in the May Day processions carried garlands. These were made of a framework of wood onto which were fixed any wild flowers and blossoms that the children could find. Some were made of two hoops, put one inside the other to make a ball shape. Some were a simple, bendable stick, bent over in a half circle. The garlands that Grey Rabbit made were crown shaped.

## THE SMALLER GARLAND

Make sure that the four sticks are placed together as in the diagram, so that the branches of the crown can come out into four corners from the centre. Bind the sticks together 40-42cm (16-17 in) from the bottom, and then about every 7.5cm (3 in) down the sticks. This will make a straight pole for you to hold. Bend the tops of the sticks out and round so they can be brought back to join onto the lower part at the top piece of tape. Tape them round securely. You should now have a crown shape on the top of a pole.

Spread the pole with glue. Wrap it round with strips of crepe paper or material. Leave it to dry. Cover the crown in the same way.

Using sticky tape, stick as many flowers as you can around the four branches of the crown,

## GREY RABBIT'S GARLAND

You will need:

4 long, straight willow branches 165-175cm (65-70 in) long, not more than 1.5cm ($\frac{1}{2}$ in) thick at the bottom end and very flexible strong sticky tape such as insulating tape or gaffer tape
glue
strips of green crepe paper or material
silk or plastic flowers

You can either make a small garland, one to be carried by one person, or a larger garland which must be threaded onto a pole or stick and carried by two people.

Whichever type you are making, first get a grown-up to cut off all the branching twigs, using secateurs. Then strip the bark from the willow sticks. You will need a penknife to do this. Hold it at an angle on the sticks and always push it away from you. If this is hard to do, get a grown-up to help.

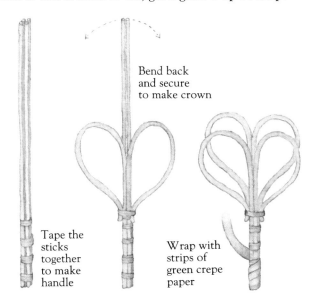

Bend back and secure to make crown

Tape the sticks together to make handle

Wrap with strips of green crepe paper

## THE LARGER GARLAND

Your willow sticks must be very bendy all the way down and it is best that you cut them as thin as possible. The four sticks should be bound together with the sticky tape about 20cm (8 in) from the bottom and again further down. Bend the tops round to meet the first piece of tape and stick them down with more tape. Decorate the garland in the same way as the small one. To carry the large garland, slide a pole through the crown. Two people will carry the pole, one on each end.

Ribbons or strips of material or coloured paper can be hung from the bottom of the crowns if you like.

## A GARLAND FROM A WIRE COAT HANGER

If you cannot find any willow branches, make your
garland like this.
You will need:

1 wire coat hanger
padding used for quilting material
strips of green material
silk or plastic flowers

Ask a grown-up to straighten the coat hanger for
you and then bend it into a half circle.

Cut the padding into strips about 5cm (2 in)
wide. Wind it round the wire, folding it over the
ends and sewing it roughly together as you go.

Cut the material into strips the same width. Wind
it round the wire and sew it onto the padding as you
do so.

Sew on the flowers. You can also put on ribbons
or strips of material.

## CROWN IMPERIALS

Hare insisted that a flower called a Crown Imperial
was placed on top of the crown garland. He walked in
front of the May Day procession carrying a single
tall flower.

Crown Imperials have stems at least 65cm (2 ft)
tall. At the top is a tuft of leaves and hanging down
from these is a circle of bright orange flowers shaped
like bells. They grow from a bulb and the flowers
come in April, just right for the May Day procession.

## THE MAY LADY

Victorian children used to dress a doll in flowers and
ribbons, hide her inside the garland and call her the
'May Lady'. They asked the rich people in the village
for 'A penny to see the May Lady' and uncovered
her when they were given the money.

A doll can be tied inside your willow garland. If
you have a coat hanger garland, tie a small basket to
the top with ribbons and put the doll in that.

This garland can either be carried by one person
with your hands about shoulder level so you can see
where you are going! Or you can have one person
holding on to each end.

# The procession

Choose a King and Queen of the May. Dress the girl
in white and the boy in green. Let them walk at the
head of the procession. All the rest must follow
behind, carrying garlands, single flowers, bunches of
flowers or branches from the May Tree. Walk along
the street or round the school or even the garden.
Stop every now and then to dance a country dance.
There are many traditional May Day songs that you
can sing as you go along. Grey Rabbit and the animals
had one of their own. Now you are ready for your
May Day procession.

*May, May, we sing to the May,*
*To sun and moon and Milky Way,*
*To field and wood and growing hay,*
*On the first of May.*

# THE CIRCUS

Grey Rabbit and her friends had no television and no radio, so when a circus came to the field near their home they hurried excitedly to see it. It was the only show that any of them had ever watched and it caused quite a stir in the countryside.

One day, why not put on your own circus? You will need at least four people.

Search the dressing-up box for things to wear or ask the grown-ups to let you have some things from their wardrobe. See if you can find a hat and a jacket for the ringmaster, something glittery for tight-rope walkers and dancers, swimsuits and tights for acrobats and weight lifters and anything that looks funny for clowns.

Paint your faces with face paints.

## The ringmaster

Choose someone with a loud voice to welcome everybody and to introduce and talk about all the different acts in the circus. Give him or her a walking stick or just a stick from the garden.

## Circus acts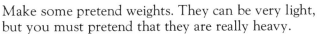

Here are a few ideas. You will probably be able to think up even better ones of your own.

### CLOWNS

Everybody loves clowns. They tell jokes, pretend to fall over things, perhaps have a pretend fight. They end up by throwing over the audience what the audience thinks is a bucket of water, only the bucket is filled with torn up newspaper instead! Watch everybody duck!

### ACROBATS

Turn head-over-heels several times, backwards and forwards across the floor. Turn cartwheels. Hold hoops for each other to jump through.

### TIGHT-ROPE WALKER

Put a plank between two up-turned buckets. Walk along it, pretending that it is much more difficult than it really is.

### WEIGHT-LIFTER

Make some pretend weights. They can be very light, but you must pretend that they are really heavy.

### CIRCUS ANIMALS

Pretend to be ponies and gallop round in a circle. Or make one person a lion tamer and two other people lions.

### JUGGLER

Play two-ball with small rubber balls or with one orange and one apple.

### MAGICIAN

Hide a paper streamer in your hand. Look in the pocket of one of the audience. Nothing is in there. Put in your hand, still hiding the streamer. Leave the streamer in the pocket, pulling one end as you take out your hand.

### GRAND FINALE

Everyone comes out and dances round the circus ring, waving to the audience.

# HAYMAKING

Squirrel, Hare and Little Grey Rabbit went haymaking on summer evenings, taking a tasty picnic with them.

Today, all the work in the farmers' fields is done with large expensive machines. But not so long ago all the work was done by hand. Men cut the grass with scythes, hooked knives fastened onto long poles. They worked steadily across the fields, swishing their scythes from side to side until all the grass lay flat.

Behind the mowers came other workers, tossing the hay up with forks and then spreading it out so that it could dry. When it was dry, the hay was raked into long lines before being tossed onto a horse drawn cart and taken back to the farmyard to be made into hay stacks or ricks. Everybody came to help, and all the children were allowed to stay away from school to get in the hay before the weather turned wet.

In good weather, haymaking was a happy time, when people enjoyed working together and sharing their meals outside. To the children, it was like a hard-working holiday, with a picnic every day.

## Let's have a picnic

Picnics are fun wherever they take place. You don't have to go on a long journey in order to have a picnic. If the weather is bad, you could even make a 'camp' in the corner of the living room!

## Picnic food

Picnic food needs to be easy to prepare, easy to carry and not too messy to eat.

SANDWICHES Use a sliced loaf, white or brown, whichever you like best, and fill them with one or more of these fillings. Marmite; mashed hard boiled egg; thin slices of cold meat; grated cheese or a cheese spread; peanut butter; jam; honey. Lettuce, watercress, slices of tomato or some mustard and cress can be put into the savoury sandwiches if you like them.

HARD BOILED EGGS Take them with the shells on.

COOKED SAUSAGES Take them in a box or a polythene bag, not on sticks, as it is safer.

SMALL SQUARES OF CHEESE

RAW VEGETABLES such as carrot or celery. Cut these into crunchy fingers.

JAM TARTS Grey Rabbit and Squirrel made raspberry tartlets for their haymaking picnic.

SMALL CAKES These are easier to carry and to serve than one large cake.

YOGHURT, or any other potted desserts.

NUTS Mix them with raisins or have them plain and eat with packets of crisps.

FRESH FRUIT that is easy to eat, such as apples, pears and grapes and small cartons of juice or home made lemonade.

Here are two of Grey Rabbit's picnic recipes:
RASPBERRY TARTLETS

You will need:
100g (4 oz) plain or wholemeal flour
pinch salt
50g (2 oz) butter
4 tablespoons cold water
12 teaspoons raspberry jam

Get a grown up to help you heat the oven to 400F/ 200C/gas 6. Put the flour and salt into a bowl. Cut the butter into small pieces. Add it to the flour and rub it in with your finger tips until you have a mixture that looks like fine breadcrumbs. Make a well in the centre. Pour in the water and mix everything to a dough.

Sprinkle some flour on a work surface and on a rolling pin. Roll out the dough. Using a 6cm (2½ in) biscuit cutter, stamp out 12 pastry rounds. Use these to line 12 patty tins. Put 1 teaspoon of jam into each one.

Bake the tarts for 15 minutes. Lift them onto a wire rack to cool.

WHAT ELSE TO TAKE
Old plates, plastic ones if you have them
Plastic beakers
Napkins for sticky fingers
A blanket to sit on
An old tablecloth to spread the food on
A bag for rubbish

LEMONADE
recipe
You will need:
2 lemons
850ml (1½ pints) water
3 tablespoons brown or white sugar or honey

Grate the yellow part only of the lemon rind and put it into a large jug. Using a sharp knife (you may feel safer if you get a grown up to help you with this), cut off all the white pithy rind from the lemons. Throw it away.

Cut the lemon flesh into thin slices. Put them into the jug. Boil the water in a kettle. Pour it into the jug. Stir in the sugar or honey.

Leave the lemonade in a cool place until it is cold. Put a sieve over a bowl. Pour the lemonade through. If it is a hot day, put it into the refrigerator, after straining, for 1 hour.

Carry the lemonade in a plastic vacuum flask.

CARRYING YOUR FOOD
Plastic boxes and polythene bags are the best containers. Pack them all into a bag or basket to take out. Put the squashiest things on top!

# SUMMER FLOWERS

Many flowers grew round Grey Rabbit's house in summer. She loved looking at them, playing with them and putting them to good use around the house. Walk through woodland, across fields, down a country lane, in your garden or round the edges of a park or playing field and see how many different kinds you can find. Here are some to look out for.

### DAISIES
Daisies grow in low grass and love lawns and playing fields. Make a daisy chain.

### FOXGLOVES
The large, pink flowers of the foxgloves can be used as finger puppets.

### CLOVER
Search amongst the leaves for a lucky four-leaved clover. Press it so that you will be able to keep it.

### WILD THYME
You can chop this and both leaves and flowers can be sprinkled over lamb chops or into stews before they are cooked. It will give them a taste of the country. You can also dry it to use in the winter. Moldy Warp used dried wild thyme as tobacco.

### WILD MARJORAM
This is a wild herb like wild thyme that you can use to flavour savoury things.

### HEATHER
To make a good luck present, pick a spray of heather. Bind it together with a rubber band. Wrap kitchen foil or silver paper round the ends of the stems to cover them and the rubber band.

## ROSE PETALS

Collect these and dry them to make pot pourri.

## MEADOWSWEET

This grows in damp places. Dry a sprig and hang it in your wardrobe to give it a sweet smell. You can also soak the flowers in a cold drink, such as lemonade or fruit juice, to give a taste of honey.

## POPPY

To make a poppy doll, pick a large poppy. Fold back the petals and tie them down over the stem with a strong piece of grass, leaving long pieces on either side of the knot for arms. Using a fine, felt tipped pen, draw a face on the seed head.

## SEA LAVENDER

This grows by muddy estuaries. Dry it to use in dried flower arrangements.

## LAVENDER

This grows in gardens. To make lavender "bottles", cut twenty flowering lavender stalks, all the same length. Tie them together just under the flowers. Bend the stalks back over the flowers, spacing them evenly, to make a kind of basket with the flowers inside. Tie the stalks again, close to the flowers. Hang the bottles in a cool, dry, airy place to dry. Tie them round with lavender coloured ribbons. Hang them in wardrobes to scent your clothes.

# SUMMER CRAFTS

## Drying flowers and herbs

Flowers and herbs that you can dry include wild thyme, wild marjoram, lavender, sea lavender, marigolds, woodruff, knapweed, scabious, the seed heads of poppies and of honesty as well as rose buds and rose petals. In your garden you can also grow a flower called helichrysum, or straw daisy, especially for drying.

Cut your flowers on a dry day, in late morning. Tie them together with string in small bunches of about six flowers.

Hang them up in a cool, dry, airy place, not in the kitchen or bathroom as these are too steamy. They are dry when the flowers and leaves feel crisp and the stalks will snap easily.

Rose petals cannot be hung up. To dry these you need a wire cake cooling rack and some kitchen paper. Spread a layer of the kitchen paper over the rack. Put on your rose petals, without letting them overlap. Cover them lightly with more kitchen paper.

## What you can do with dried flowers

The prettiest flowers and seed heads can be used in flower arrangements. Some can be cut from their stems and used to make pot pourri look pretty.

The flowers and leaves of the herbs should be rubbed off their stems and stored in dark coloured, air-tight jars and containers until you need to use them. Lavender flowers and rose petals should be stored in the same way.

# Make lavender bags

For one lavender bag you will need:
two pieces flower patterned cotton material, 7.5cm × 13cm
(3in × 5 in)
sewing thread to match the material
15cm (6 in) piece narrow ribbon to match the material
lavender flowers

Put right sides together

Leave this side open

Sew around three sides

Turn in
3.8cm (1½ in)
of raw edge

3.2cm (1¼ in)

Run gathering stitch
all round bag

Turn bag right way out

Put the right sides of the pieces of material together.
Sew round three sides in a 1cm (⅜ in) seam, leaving
a short side open. Trim the corners. Turn the bag right
way out and press it. Turn in 4cm (1½ in) of
the raw edge. Press again. Run a gathering stitch all
round the bag, 3.5cm (1¼ in) from the top.

Fill the bag with dried lavender flowers to just below
the gathering stitch. Pull up the gathers and tie them.
Tie the ribbon round the gathers. Tie it in a bow if it is
to be put in a drawer, or make a long loop with it if the
bag is to be hung on a coat hanger.

# Make bouquets garnis

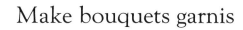

*" . . . a bowl of nettle broth, flavoured with wild marjoram and cloves . . ."*

These are little bags of cooking herbs. Make them with your dried wild herbs, or, if you do not have any, you can buy dried herbs from a shop. Give bouquets garnis as a present to someone who loves cooking. They are put into soups, stews and casseroles to give them flavour and taken out before they are served.

*To make one bouquet garni you will need:*
a circle of thin muslin 11.5cm (4½ in) across (you can buy muslin in any good material shop)
cream coloured cotton thread
1 tablespoon mixed dried wild marjoram and wild thyme
15cm (6 in) fine cotton string

Gather all the way round the circle of muslin 2.5cm (1 in) from the edge. Pull up the gathers, about half way, to make a small bag that is easy to fill. Put the herbs inside the bag. Pull up the gathers tightly and tie them. Trim off the long threads. Tie the string round the gathers, making a long loop.

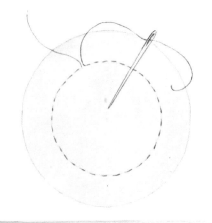

# An easy pot pourri to make

A pot pourri is a mixture of dried flowers and spices. It is kept in a bowl to give a sweet scent to a room. You will have to buy some of the ingredients. For the special ingredients, go to a place that sells dried herbs and flowers or to a good chemist. The spices can be bought in supermarkets, grocers, delicatessens and health shops.

You will need:

25g (1 oz) dried rose petals
25g (1 oz) dried lavender flowers
1 tablespoon dried wild marjoram (or dried marjoram from a shop)
1 tablespoon dried wild thyme (or ordinary thyme from a shop)
1 teaspoon allspice berries
1 teaspoon cloves
1 tablespoon orris root powder
4 drops rose oil (these last two ingredients are the special ones)

Put the dried flowers and herbs into a bowl. Crush the spices together. Use a pestle and mortar for this, or put them between two pieces of paper and crush them with a rolling pin. Mix them into the flowers and herbs. Mix in the orris root powder. Add the rose oil very carefully, for it smells very strong if you add too much. Mix well.

Put the pot pourri into a polythene bag and seal it with a tie. Leave it for 6 weeks, shaking it every other day.

Put the pot pourri into a bowl. If you have any pretty dried flowers arrange a few on the top so the pot pourri will be pretty as well as sweet smelling.

# AUTUMN

At the beginning of autumn, Grey Rabbit, Squirrel and Hare went out with their baskets and bags to look for nuts and berries for their winter store.

They knew that the nights were soon going to get longer, so they also picked rushes to make rush lights and collected seeds and conkers and other things that they could use to make presents and toys during the long winter evenings.

Grey Rabbit stocked up her medicine cupboard in case anyone caught a winter chill. Hare made sure that they had enough firewood to keep the kitchen fire going until spring.

## RUSH LIGHTS and CANDLES

There was no electric light in Grey Rabbit's house and so she and her friends had to make sure that they made enough rush lights and candles to light the house through the dark days of winter.

You can make them, too. Candles and rush lights give a beautiful soft light, and it is surprising how bright it can be.

### Rush lights

You will need to go for a walk in a damp, boggy place in September to find rushes for making rush lights. The plant you want is called the Soft Rush and its Latin name is *Juncus effusus*. It has a long, smooth glossy stem which can be up to one metre (3 ft) long. The stems have a tuft of small brown flowers towards the top and no leaves, and they grow in spiky clumps. Using scissors so you do not damage the plant, pick the thickest ones, as long as you can.

When you get them home, cut the rushes into lengths about 30cm (12 in).

Now comes the tricky part. You have to carefully peel away the outer green part of the stems, leaving a stick of white pith. This pith is very fragile so you may find that you will break several rushes before you are able to peel a whole one successfully. If your rushes keep breaking, do not worry too much. Even short lengths of about 10cm (4 in) can be used.

When your rushes are peeled, with a grown-up's help, put some pure lard into a frying pan, and gently melt it. If you bought some rose oil in the summer to make a pot pourri you can also add a few drops of this to make the lights smell sweet as they burn.

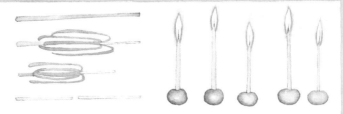

Roll the rushes in the lard. Lift them out and lay them on a tray until they are cool and hard. Store them by wrapping them in kitchen paper and putting them into a polythene bag.

In country cottages, there used to be special rush light holders, but yours will burn just as well if you mould a steady base of plasticene round each one so that the light can stand upright. Carefully light it with a match.

The flame will be long and bright and steady, but you will find your light burns down far more quickly than candles, so you should have another ready to light when the first has burned down.

## Making rolled candles

This is an easy, safe way to make your own candles as you do not need to melt the wax.

You will need:

Sheets of honeycombed beeswax: You can either buy these from a local beekeeper (who puts them in his hives to help the bees build up small compartments for the queen to lay her eggs in) or you can buy them from shops specialising in candlemaking equipment. The sheets are usually about 20cm × 34cm (8in × 13½ in).

A length of 4cm (1½ in) wick. (4cm [1½ in] is the width of candle for which the wick is suitable. It is nearly always used for beeswax candles.) This can be bought from shops specialising in candle making equipment.

You can make tall candles by using the whole of the sheet of beeswax, or short ones by cutting sheets of wax in half lengthways. The height of the candle will be the measurement of the shorter side, either 20cm (8 in) or 10cm (4 in).

Cut a length of wick 2.5cm (1 in) longer than the height of the candle. Lay it on the edge of one narrow side of your wax, allowing about 2cm (¾ in) at the end of which will be the top of the candle. Carefully fold the edge of the wax over it, easing it with your fingers. Begin to roll up the wax round the wick, as tightly as you can. This gets easier as the candle gets fatter.

To seal the loose end of the wax, warm a round ended knife over a hot plate (you may wish to get a grown-up to help you do this). Run the knife down the end of the wax and quickly press the wax down to seal it to the rest of the candle. Using a warmed sharp knife cut the top of the candle into a point.

Trim the wick to about 1cm (½ in) long at the top and, if necessary, cut it level with the base of the candle.

Beeswax candles give off the smell of honey as they burn.

# FRUITS, NUTS and BERRIES

In early autumn, Grey Rabbit and all the other woodland animals collected food for their winter store. It is fun to go out finding good things to eat.

While you are searching, make sure that no one minds your being in their fields or woods; and never take more than you need. Remember the animals need these things to keep them going during the winter.

## Blackberries

Everybody loves blackberries and they are fun to pick as long as you wear boots to keep your legs and feet from being scratched. Put them with apples into a pie or crumble.

SIMMERED BLACKBERRIES
   You will need:
225g (8 oz) blackberries
2 tablespoons honey
2 tablespoons red grape juice or apple juice

Put the blackberries, honey and grape juice into a saucepan. Ask a grown-up to help you to turn on a hot plate to a low heat. Put the saucepan on the heat and put on the lid. Cook the blackberries for about 10 minutes, or until they are juicy. Take the saucepan off the heat and cool the blackberries. Eat them with cream or evaporated milk.

## Sloes

These are like purple plums and are the fruits of the blackthorn bush. If you know someone making plum jam or jelly, or even apple jelly, ask them to put in some sloes. They will give a deep purple colour and extra fruity flavour. They are not very nice to eat raw.

## Hazelnuts

Hazel trees can be found in woods and alongside hedgerows. Do not pick too many as the squirrels like them, too.

Fresh hazelnuts are easy to crack and the nuts are crisp and white and fresh tasting.

Eat them with dates or raisins or with cheese and put them into salads with celery and apples.

## Crab apples

These grow on trees in woods and along hedgerows. You can also find them on heathland. You may have a crab apple tree in your garden.

SPICED BAKED CRAB APPLES
   You will need:
225g (8 oz) crab apples
15g (½ oz) butter
100g (4 oz) dark brown sugar

Get a grown-up to help you heat the oven to 350F/180C/gas 4. Cut the crab apples into lengthways quarters. Cut out the small pieces of core and throw them away. Do not peel.

Put the butter into a small casserole or ovenproof dish. Put in the crab apples. Mix in the sugar. Cover the casserole and put it into the oven for 45 minutes. Give the apples a good stir. Serve hot or cold, with thick yoghurt or spooned over ice-cream.

## Sweet chestnuts

Sweet chestnuts are ready in November after they have fallen from the trees and their prickly shells have split.

Grey Rabbit enjoyed eating roasted chestnuts. To prepare them, first get a grown-up to help you turn on the oven to 400F/200C/gas 6. Then, using a sharp knife, make a slit in the top of each chestnut. Put the chestnuts onto a baking tray. Put them into the oven for 15 minutes. Leave them for a few minutes to cool down and then peel away the shells and eat the soft insides.

# Rose hips

Rose hips are the fruit of the wild rose. They are a bright orangy-red and can be found along the hedgerows. Rose hip syrup is a delicious drink, full of goodness to help keep away winter colds.

ROSE HIP SYRUP

You will need:
450g (1 lb) rose hips
1.3 litres ($2\frac{1}{4}$ pints) water
225g (8 oz) sugar for every
425ml ($\frac{3}{4}$ pint) strained liquid

Put 725ml ($1\frac{1}{4}$ pints) water into a saucepan. Get a grown-up to help you to bring it to the boil on top of the stove. Mince the rosehips or chop them finely in a food processor. Put them into the boiling water. Let the water boil again. Take the saucepan off the heat and leave it for 15 minutes.

Line a colander with an old linen tea towel. Place the colander over a bowl. Strain the rosehips through into the bowl, without pressing down on the cloth.

Carefully take the cloth of rosehips away and put the rosehips back into the saucepan. Boil the rest of the water in another saucepan. Pour it over the rosehips. Give them a good stir and leave them for 10 minutes.

Put the cloth into the colander again. Strain the water from the rosehips into the first batch.

Clean out the saucepan. Using a measuring jug, find out how many pints of liquid you have. Put it into the cleaned saucepan. Add the right amount of sugar (get a grown-up to help you work it out if it is hard). Stir on a low heat until the sugar has dissolved. Boil the syrup for 5 minutes.

Carefully pour the syrup into clean, warmed bottles. To drink the syrup, dilute it with hot or cold water, like squash.

# Things to make in Autumn

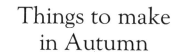

Look around the countryside in the autumn and collect conkers, seeds, nut shells and other things to take home to make into toys.

## Conkers

These fall from the horse chestnut tree in October.

To make conker dolls, you will need large and small conkers and a supply of used matchsticks plus a bodkin or fine skewer to make holes in the conkers. Use large conkers for bodies, small ones for heads and the matchsticks for arms and legs and also, broken in half, to join the bodies and heads together. Acorns, cut in half, can be used for feet. Animals can be made in the same way.

To make a dolls' house chair, find a flat shaped conker. Stick in four matchsticks for the legs and two more side by side in the top of the conker for the back. Wind wool or string round these two to fill in the back of the chair.

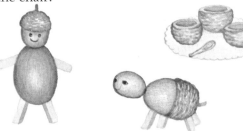

## Acorns

You can make animals and people with these in the same ways as with conkers. If you use ones with the cups still attached for the heads, your people will have hats.

To make an acorn necklace, thread a thick needle with strong button thread and use it to string the acorns on the thread.

Acorn cups can be used in a dolls' house as bowls.

# Lime seeds

The small seeds of the lime tree are prettily patterned in ridges and make ideal necklaces. As with the acorns, use strong button thread and a thick needle for threading. If you have a spindle tree in your garden, put one of its pink seeds onto the thread to every three lime seeds. Their colour will change from pink to dark red but the necklace will be very pretty.

# Walnut shells

To crack a walnut to give you two complete half shells, do not squeeze the nut crackers too hard. After you hear the first crack, do not use the crackers any more, but gradually ease the two halves apart with your finger nails.

To make a boat with a walnut shell, put a little blob of Plasticine into the shell. Cut out a small paper sail. Stick a used matchstick through the sail and then into the Plasticene.

For a basket of flowers, again put Plasticine into the shell. Stick dried flowers into the Plasticine to cover it completely.

To make a tiny doll's cradle, cut two pieces of material 2.5cm × 2cm (1 in × $\frac{3}{4}$ in). Sew them together round three sides, put a small piece of cotton wool between them and sew up the remaining side. This is the pillow. Do the same with two pieces 3cm (1$\frac{1}{4}$ in) square for the cover, and cut a single sheet 2.5cm (1 in) square.

# Beech nut casings

To make a dancing lady, make a 1cm ($\frac{3}{8}$ in) loop in the centre of a pipe cleaner. Hold it against the stem of the upturned beech nut case. Twist each end of the pipe cleaner around the stem. The loop will be the head and the ends of the pipe cleaners the arms, cut them to the right size with scissors.

For a dried flower arrangement, get a piece of oasis 2cm ($\frac{3}{4}$ in) thick and 5cm (2 in) round. Stick in a mixture of beech nut cases and dried flowers. Press a small piece of Plasticine into each beech nut case and press a small dried flower into it.

# Teasels

To make Mrs Hedgehog you will need two circles of pretty material, one 23cm (9 in) in diameter and the other 18cm (7 in). Turn in and sew 6mm ($\frac{1}{4}$ in) round each one. Run a gathering stitch 1cm ($\frac{1}{2}$ in) from the edge of each finished circle. Pull up the gathers of the largest circle to make a bag and tie them securely. Stuff the bag with old tights, cotton wool or special toy stuffing. You can also put in some dried lavender.

Cut a teasel with a 4cm ($1\frac{1}{2}$ in) stem. Bend the head at right angles to the stem. Put some glue on the top of the stuffing. Push the stem of the teasel down into the stuffing and push the head onto the glue to secure it.

Pull up the gathers on the second circle to make the hat. Put the hat on the teasel. The prickles should keep it in place. Use pins with round coloured ends for the eyes and nose. Push these into the face when the glue is dry.

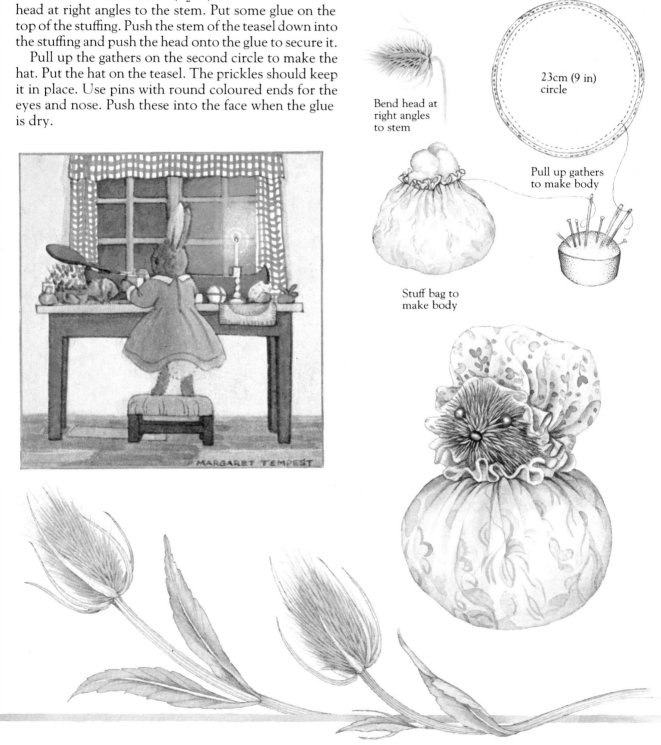

18cm (7 in) circle

Pull up gathers to make hat

Bend head at right angles to stem

23cm (9 in) circle

Pull up gathers to make body

Stuff bag to make body

MARGARET TEMPEST

# To make a sheep's wool pillow

Grey Rabbit and Squirrel collected sheep's wool from fences and hedges, washed it, spun it and used it for spinning or knitting. You can use it for stuffing a pillow for a doll's pram or cradle.

You will need:

50g (2 oz) ball Aran knitting wool (this will make two but you will have to buy this amount)

15g ($\frac{1}{2}$ oz) sheep's wool (like Grey Rabbit, you can collect this from the fences around fields where sheep have been grazing)

Size 4mm (old size 8) knitting needles

Cast on 30 stitches. Knit until your work measures 12.5cm (5 in). Cast off. Knit another piece the same size. With right sides together, sew the pieces round three sides. Turn the bag. Fill it with sheep's wool. Sew up the remaining side.

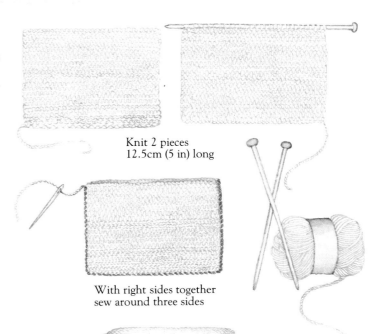

Knit 2 pieces
12.5cm (5 in) long

With right sides together
sew around three sides

Turn the bag
Fill with sheep's wool
Sew up remaining side

# Fallen leaves

To make a leaf print, paint the rough side of a leaf with thick paint. Press the leaf, paint side down, onto a clean sheet of paper. Take the leaf away and the shape and pattern of the leaf will be on the paper. You can make your own wrapping paper in this way.

# PATCHWORK

Wise Owl sent Grey Rabbit a book called 'How to Make a Coat out of Bits and Pieces'. Hare collected scraps of material from all the neighbouring animals. Then he and Grey Rabbit and Squirrel sat round the table making a patchwork coat for Brush, the Wandering Hedgehog. Here is how to make patchwork.

You will need:

Small piece thick cardboard
Thin cardboard or thick paper
Scraps all the same thickness, but different colours that go well together
Pins
Sharp scissors
Needle and cotton

## MAKING THE SHAPES

First, trace this shape onto thick cardboard

Cut out the shape. This cardboard cut-out is called a template. Put your template onto the thin card or thick paper and draw round it. Do this seven times and cut out the shapes. Keep the template for another time.

## CUTTING OUT

Pin your paper shapes onto the wrong side of your material, leaving a 1cm ($\frac{3}{8}$ in) gap all round each one. Cut out your material, making the material pieces 1cm ($\frac{3}{8}$ in) bigger all round than the paper pieces. Leave the paper pinned to the material.

## TACKING

Fold the extra width of the material back over the paper. Tack the corners together, sewing only through the material, not the paper. Take out the pins.

## ARRANGING THE PATTERN

Your seven pieces of material will together make a flower shape. Choose one to be the centre of the flower. Lay it on a table, right side up. Arrange the other pieces round it in the places that you want them to be when the shape is finished.

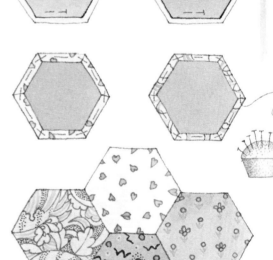

## SEWING TOGETHER

Pick up the centre piece (1). Put it right sides together with one of the side pieces (2). Sew them together along one edge using tiny oversewing stitches, taking care not to stick the needle through the paper. Make sure that the ends are fastened off securely. Take up the patch that is to be opposite the first outside patch in the finished flower shape (3). In the same way, sew it to the opposite side of the centre piece. Lay these three joined pieces back down with the others.

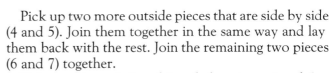

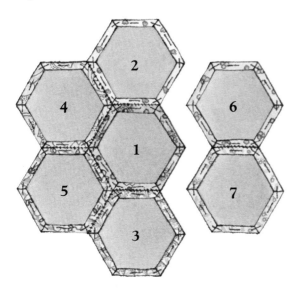

Pick up two more outside pieces that are side by side (4 and 5). Join them together in the same way and lay them back with the rest. Join the remaining two pieces (6 and 7) together.

Take up pieces 1, 2 and 3 and also pieces 4 and 5. Sew 4 to pieces 1 and 2 and piece 5 to pieces 1 and 3. Then, for the other side, join piece 6 to pieces 1 and 2 and piece 7 to pieces 1 and 3. Be careful to match the corners and joins exactly so you finish with a smooth, even shaped flower.

### FINISHING
Remove the pieces of paper. Get a grown up to help you press your patchwork flat.

# Making a patchwork cover

Make more patchwork flowers and join them all together to make a small coverlet. Join them together with the same oversewing stitch. You can also fill in gaps at the edges with single pieces of material. When all the pieces are joined, take out the tacking stitches and press the finished cover.

Or, your single patchwork flower can be used to decorate things made with plain material. Here are some ideas for where to put it:

shoe-bag
apron
cushion cover
sweat-shirt

# Sewing patchwork to plain material

Pin the patchwork in place. Slip stitch all round it using tiny stitches that hardly show. Take out the tacking cottons. Press the patchwork and the material that it is sewn on to.

# AUTUMN BONFIRES

Hare heard about Bonfire Night from Robin the postman so he swept fallen leaves into a heap and collected wood to make a bonfire. There are autumn leaves and hedge trimmings and all other kinds of garden rubbish to burn.

## Building a bonfire

When you are planning your bonfire, make sure that you build it in a safe place, away from the house, garden sheds and hedges, and do not make it too big for the space that it is in.

Start off with very dry, easily burnable things, such as screwed up newspaper, cardboard boxes, dry leaves, old pea sticks and dry hedge trimmings. Then gradually build the larger sticks and branches round these, always leaning their tops inwards towards the centre.

Always get a grown-up to light the bonfire for you and stay near it while it is alight.

## Bonfire food

Hare made treacle toffee to eat on Bonfire Night and Grey Rabbit and Squirrel made Parkin which was once a traditional bonfire treat in the North of England. The animals also baked potatoes in the embers of the fire, but it is much easier to put them in the oven while you are enjoying your bonfire and come back into the kitchen to eat them afterwards.

POTATOES IN THEIR JACKETS
You will need:

1 large potato per person
butter to serve with them

Scrub the potatoes. Prick them twice on both sides with a fork. Put them into the oven. Get a grown-up to turn the oven on to 400F/200C/gas 6. Leave the potatoes for 1 hour 30 minutes. Get a grown-up to take them out of the oven. Cut them in half and put on knobs of butter.

## HARE'S BONFIRE TOFFEE

You will need:

300g (10oz) Demerara sugar
2 tablespoons black treacle
2 tablespoons honey
100g (4oz) butter, cut into small pieces,
plus more for greasing the tins
4 tablespoons water

Butter two 15cm (6 in) shallow tins. Put all the ingredients into a saucepan. Get a grown-up to help you turn a hot plate onto a low heat and help you test when the toffee is ready. It will be very hot so you must be careful.

Put the saucepan of ingredients onto the low heat and stir them until they have dissolved together. Turn the heat to medium and bring them to the boil. Cover the saucepan and let the toffee boil for 2 minutes.

Take off the lid and boil the toffee for 10-15 minutes, stirring occasionally. It will be ready to pour out when a teaspoon of toffee dropped into a saucepan of very cold water gets hard very quickly and snaps when you bend it. (If you have a sugar thermometer, it should read 300F/149C.)

Pour the toffee into the tins. Cool it slightly and then score it into small squares while it is still soft. Leave it until it is cold and hard. Turn it out of the tins.

## GREY RABBIT'S PARKIN

Make this several days ahead and store it, cut up, in a polythene bag. The longer you keep it, the more moist it will become.

You will need:

300g (10 oz) plain flour
175g (6 oz) fine oatmeal
1 teaspoon ground ginger
1 teaspoon ground mixed spice
2 teaspoons bicarbonate of soda
175g (6 oz) butter, cut into small pieces, plus extra for greasing
225g (8 oz) honey
225g (8 oz) black treacle

Butter a 20cm × 28cm (8 in × 11 in), 5cm (2 in) deep cake tin. Get a grown-up to heat the oven to 350F/180C/gas 4.

Put the flour, ginger, mixed spice and bicarbonate of soda into a large bowl. Toss them together and make a well in the centre. Put the butter, honey and treacle into a saucepan. Get a grown-up to put the

saucepan on a low heat. Stir until everything has dissolved. Pour the mixture into the well of flour and spices. Mix everything together well. Pour the mixture into the cake tin.

Bake the parkin for 40 minutes, or until a skewer stuck into the middle comes out clean. Turn the parkin onto a wire rack to get cold. Cut it into squares.

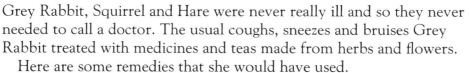
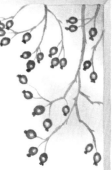

# GREY RABBIT'S MEDICINE CUPBOARD

Grey Rabbit, Squirrel and Hare were never really ill and so they never needed to call a doctor. The usual coughs, sneezes and bruises Grey Rabbit treated with medicines and teas made from herbs and flowers. Here are some remedies that she would have used.

BLACKCURRANT TEA for colds. Put a tablespoon of blackcurrant jam into a mug. Pour on hot water and stir. You could also use blackcurrant cordial.

SAGE TEA for sore throats. Make it like ordinary tea, using fresh or dried sage leaves. Do not add milk, but honey or sugar.

ELDERFLOWER TEA for the beginnings of a cold. Use fresh or dried elderflowers.

PEPPERMINT TEA for an upset tummy. Use peppermint tea bags.

HONEY
Many people say that honey is good for colds. You can add a teaspoon of honey to sage or elderflower tea, or make a honey and lemon drink by putting a teaspoon of honey and the juice of a lemon into a mug and pouring on hot water.

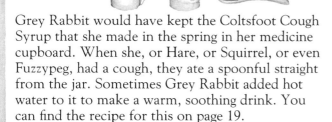

Grey Rabbit would have kept the Coltsfoot Cough Syrup that she made in the spring in her medicine cupboard. When she, or Hare, or Squirrel, or even Fuzzypeg, had a cough, they ate a spoonful straight from the jar. Sometimes Grey Rabbit added hot water to it to make a warm, soothing drink. You can find the recipe for this on page 19.

When Grey Rabbit had a cold she bandaged her neck with soft mullein leaves. You can use a scarf that you have warmed on the radiator.
Grey Rabbit used dock leaves to rub on bruises. Most country children use them to rub on nettle stings.
Working outside during the winter might well have given Grey Rabbit and her friends chapped hands. Here is a lotion to make them feel better.

You will need:

125ml (4fl oz) rose water
4 tablespoons glycerine (both these can be bought from a chemist)

Put the rose water and glycerine into a bottle. Put the top on tight. Shake the bottle hard to mix the rose water and glycerine together.

# THE FIRESIDE

In the long, cold evenings of autumn and winter, Grey Rabbit and her friends gathered round the fire to tell tales and sing songs. Grey Rabbit's oven was heated by a fire and Fuzzypeg enjoyed toasting muffins in front of it.

## Toasting

If you are lucky enough to have an open fire in your house, you can use it to toast bread, muffins and crumpets and have them for tea on a cold winter's afternoon. You will need a special toasting fork that has a long handle that will not melt or get too hot. Stick your slice of bread or your muffin onto the fork and hold it close to the flames. When it has browned, turn it over and toast the other side. Spread it with butter and eat it while it is hot. Toast made in this way has a special, smoky flavour and even if you burn the edges it still manages to taste good!

MUFFINS
You may need some help from an adult to make these muffins, but kneading the dough can be great fun.

You will need:

450g (1 lb) strong white flour, or wholemeal flour, or half and half
1 teaspoon salt
25g (1 oz) fresh yeast or 15g ($\frac{1}{2}$ oz) dried
$\frac{1}{2}$ pint milk, warmed
1 teaspoon sugar, if you are using dried yeast

Put the flour and salt into a large mixing bowl. If you are using fresh yeast, crumble it into a small bowl and pour on the milk. Add it to the bread straightaway. If you have dried yeast, dissolve the sugar in the milk and sprinkle in the yeast. Leave the mixture in a warm place until it is frothy.

Pour the yeast mixture into the flour and mix it in. Turn the dough onto a floured board or work top. Flour your hands and knead the dough until it feels smooth and no longer sticks to your hands. Put the dough back into the large bowl and cut a cross in the top. Cover it with a clean tea cloth and leave it in a warm place for 1 hour or until it has grown to twice its size. Turn it onto the floured work top again and knead it. It will not be so sticky this time. Make the dough into 12 round, flat muffins.

Lightly grease a heavy frying pan or, if you have one, a griddle. Get a grown-up to put it on a medium heat for you. Put on as many muffins as will fit and cook them until they are light brown on each side. Cook the other muffins. Put them all on a wire rack to cool.

MARGARET TEMPEST

Do not cut your muffins in half for toasting. They must be toasted whole, so the inside stays soft. When both sides have been crisped by the fire, cut them open and spread them with plenty of butter and then with jam or honey.

## Stories and songs

One evening, pretend that your television is not in the room. If you have an open fire, gather round that. If not, you can still arrange your chairs in a circle so that you talk to one another.

If you have a fire, look at the changing shapes. What can you see? A castle? A forest? Can you make up a story together about them? See if you can. If you don't have a fire, try the game of one person starting to tell a story and breaking off in an interesting part so the next person has to carry on.

You can sing songs round your fire, too. You can each sing a song in turn, or, if you are not brave enough, sing some rounds so that everyone can join in together and yet each sing their own particular part. If you play a recorder or another instrument, you could play a tune instead.

# WINTER

Winter is a happy season. Jack Frost paints pictures on your windows in the night and when the snow comes you can wrap up warm and go sledging.

The best part of winter is Christmas. Grey Rabbit decorated her house with holly and ivy and made mince pies for everyone. On Christmas Eve the carol singers came to call and on Christmas Day, Grey Rabbit and Squirrel and Hare enjoyed themselves eating and drinking and pulling crackers. In the evening they went to visit Moldy Warp who decorated a tree and provided food for all his animal friends.

## SKATING and SLEDGING

Winter snow and ice can be great fun. Hare was so excited when he heard from Old Hedgehog that the ponds had frozen, that he gobbled up his breakfast as fast as he could, so that he should not miss the skating. Later on, just before Christmas, Grey Rabbit asked Old Joe the Carpenter to make her a bright scarlet sledge so that she and Squirrel and Hare could ride down their favourite hill on it.

Whichever outdoor sport you choose, wrap up warm, put on something waterproof if you have it and also several pairs of socks. You don't want to get chilblains like Hare! To keep your hands warm and dry, put on gloves and, over the top, a polythene bag anchored down with an elastic band.

# Sledging

You can buy plain wooden sledges from garden centres and hardware shops. Why not paint yours red and put your name on it, like Grey Rabbit? You can also buy plastic sledges which are already bright colours, but you can still paint your name on them. If you have no sledge you can use a large, thick, empty plastic bag, such as a coal bag or fertiliser or animal feed bag. Sit on it and hold the end up between your legs to help you stay on.

Go up to the top of a hill, make sure there is nothing in your way, push yourself off, and away you go!

# Skating

If you are lucky enough to own skates and wish to use them outside, always let a grown-up test the ice first to make sure that it is safe, and make sure that you are never on your own.

# Food for winter games

Grey Rabbit took sandwiches and hot lemonade when the animals went skating. You can make the lemonade that you took on the summer picnic. Strain it, warm it up and put it into a vacuum flask.

Soup is lovely and warming after you have been playing in the snow. Make a tomato and green pea soup by mixing a tin of tomato soup and a tin of pea soup in a saucepan. Stir as you warm them up and pour your soup into a vacuum flask.

When the nights are very cold, you may well wake up in the morning to find that Jack Frost has painted icy pictures on your windows. Grey Rabbit saw trees, ferns and flowers painted in silver on her windows. What do the patterns on your windows look like?

# To make a Jack Frost picture

You will need:

a sheet of dark coloured paper, black or dark blue are best
a pencil or a silver crayon
a glue stick
a packet of silver glitter

Using a pencil or a crayon, draw a picture on the paper. This could be a ferny, flowery pattern like the pictures on your windows, or a winter scene, perhaps with Jack Frost actually painting the windows.

Now go over your drawing with the glue stick. While the glue is still sticky, sprinkle the glitter over it. Shake off the extra glitter when the glue is dry.

# CHRISTMAS EVERGREENS

At Christmas time and for their winter party, Grey Rabbit, Squirrel and Hare decorated their house with holly and mistletoe.

For many centuries evergreen branches were the only decoration people had in their houses and churches.

In the depths of winter, they were a sign that the earth was not dead but sleeping, and more green leaves would come in the spring.

The thick leaves of evergreens do not wither indoors and so they make ideal Christmas decorations. It is supposed to be unlucky, though, to leave them up after Twelfth Night, 6th January.

Even if you have a lot of paper and tinsel decorations, put evergreens among them to set them off.

## HOLLY

Holly trees were once planted in gardens as they were said to protect houses from thunder and lightning, fire and witches. Sometimes a piece was put over the cowshed door to make the cows thrive.

It was thought unlucky to burn green holly or to stamp on the berries.

Holly wood is hard and lasts a long time and so it is often made into walking sticks.

Put sprigs of holly over picture frames and lay them along book shelves.

## IVY

Ivy was another plant that was thought to protect houses from witches and evil spirits.

Use both the leaves and the dark blue berries of ivy alongside holly.

## ROSEMARY

We mostly think of rosemary as a herb now, but it was once left to grow very large so that sprigs could be picked for Christmas decorations. Rosemary was said to be a holy and magical plant that bloomed at midnight on Christmas Eve.

Small sprigs of rosemary look good in arrangements of both fresh and dried flowers.

## MISTLETOE

Like holly, mistletoe was said to keep the house safe from thunder and lightning and the spells of witches.

In Scandinavia it was the plant of peace, hospitality and welcome, but the custom of kissing under the mistletoe is an English one.

Mistletoe grows on a number of trees including apple, hawthorn and willow, but it is said to be most magical when it grows on oak.

Mistletoe is often hung from the ceiling in small bunches by itself.

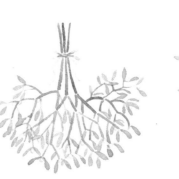

## LAUREL

If you have a laurel tree in your garden, use some branches of this with your holly and mistletoe. The large, shiny leaves stay fresh for a long time after they have been cut. Both laurel and bay were once used for decorating churches.

## CUTTING EVERGREENS

Evergreen branches are usually very tough and so you will need secateurs or strong scissors with which to cut them. Get a grown-up to help you. Tie several branches together with string so that you can carry them easily.

Do not cut all your branches from the same tree, or you will not be able to cut any from it the following year. Protect the trees by cutting only one or two branches from each one.

# Putting up your evergreens

It was once thought unlucky to bring evergreens into the house before Christmas Eve. Do not bring them in too soon or they will be past their best on Christmas Day and the days immediately after.

Remember to take all your decorations down by Twelfth Night, 6th January.

# THE KISSING BUNCH

Grey Rabbit twisted sprays of holly together to make a round ball called a Kissing Bunch. She hung it from a hook in the ceiling and she, Squirrel and Hare stood under it to give each other their Christmas kisses.

The Kissing Bunch took pride of place in our homes before we had Christmas trees. Now we can have both.

## Make a kissing bunch

You will need:

7.5cm (3 in) diameter ball of Oasis (the type used for dried flowers)
1m (40 in) red ribbon, 1.5cm ($\frac{5}{8}$ in) wide
40 sprigs holly about 18cm (7 in) long
40 sprigs ivy about 18cm (7 in) long
About 12 small shiny glass balls with wire stems. These are often used in Christmas flower arrangements and you can buy them from flower shops and some department stores. Choose red, gold or silver or a selection.

Cut the ends of the ribbon into V-shapes to stop them fraying. Fold the ribbon in half. Using a narrow skewer or a knitting needle, pierce the Oasis from top to bottom, then push the two ends of the ribbon together through the Oasis, using the same skewer or knitting needle, and holding the ribbon to the skewer with sticky tape. Pull them down, still holding the ends together, until the loop at the top of the ball measures 25cm (10 in). Knot the two ends of the ribbon together twice.

Stick the sprigs of holly and ivy into the ball at regular intervals. Wind the stems of the shiny balls round the holly and ivy sprigs, making sure that the balls will show when the kissing bunch is hung up.

If your holly has no berries, you can buy artificial berries which you wind round the stems.

You can use narrow red ribbon to tie bows here and there on the kissing bunch to add extra colour.

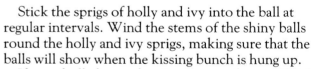

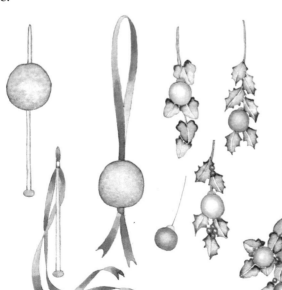

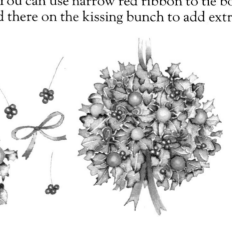

52

# CHRISTMAS CRACKERS

Grey Rabbit, Squirrel and Hare pulled crackers on Christmas Day. You can make your own crackers and use them as an unusual way of wrapping small presents.

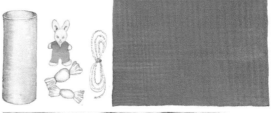

## Make crackers

You will need:

cardboard tube 11.5cm (4½ in) long
small present
1 piece red, white or green crepe paper 33cm × 15cm (13 in × 6 in)
1 piece red, white or green crepe paper (a different colour from the first) 23cm × 15cm (9 in × 6 in)
glue
thin glittery string
last year's Christmas cards to cut up

Push the present into the tube. Lay the smaller piece of paper in the centre of the larger piece. Glue them together down the two long sides, leaving 2.5cm (1 in) at each end.

Put the pieces of crepe paper onto a work surface with the larger piece uppermost. Lay the cardboard tube in the centre of one long edge. Glue it to the edge. Roll it up in the paper. Glue the paper down the second long edge to secure it over the tube.

Glue down long edges

Leave 2.5cm (1 in) unglued

Tie the paper on either side of the tube using the glittery string.

Cut down the edges of each piece of paper to make 2.5cm (1 in) frills.

Cut a small picture from a Christmas card and stick it on the cracker. If you like you can also cut a label from another card and thread it on the string before tying up the cracker. Then, if you are making several crackers, you will know who each one is for.

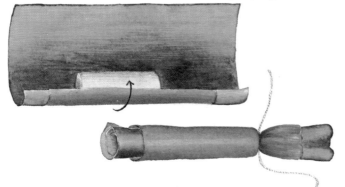

# CHRISTMAS TREE DECORATIONS

Moldy Warp put presents of food for Grey Rabbit and her friends all round his candle-lit Christmas tree.

To give your friends a surprise present from your tree, make tiny stockings and fill them with sweets or nuts and raisins.

Put the two pieces of felt together and pin on your paper shape. Cut round it.

Sew the two cut-out pieces of felt together, using a 1cm ($\frac{3}{8}$ in) seam and leaving the top open. Trim the seam and clip into the curves. Turn the stocking the right way out.

STOCKINGS

Trace this shape onto paper and cut it out

Sew the 11.5cm ($4\frac{1}{2}$ in) piece of braid, bias binding or ribbon by hand round the top of the stocking, about 6mm ($\frac{1}{4}$ in) down from the edge.

For one stocking, you will need:
two 11.5cm ($4\frac{1}{2}$ in) square pieces of red felt
11.5cm ($4\frac{1}{2}$ in) white or green bias binding or narrow ribbon or braid, or narrow silver or gold braid
10cm (4 in) red, white or green bias binding or narrow ribbon for the loop

Fold the bias binding for the loop in half lengthways to make it narrow. Then fold it in half crossways to make a loop. Sew this loop securely to the back seam of the stocking.

Now you can fill the stocking with sweets or nuts and raisins ready to hang on the tree.

LABELS

If you like you can make labels for your Christmas stockings. Cut out small pictures from last year's Christmas cards. Make a hole in the top and tie a piece of glittery string through it. Tie the string onto the stocking. This way you can make special presents for different people and not get them muddled up when they are on the tree.

# CHRISTMAS BISCUITS

Another way of decorating your tree is to make Christmas biscuits. These are crisp and spicy with a hole in the middle through which you can thread coloured ribbons to hang them on the tree.

BISCUITS

For about twenty biscuits you will need:

100g (4 oz) butter, softened
50g (2 oz) honey
175g (6 oz) wholemeal flour, plus extra for rolling out
1 teaspoon ground mixed spice
2 large bowls
wooden spoon
rolling pin
pastry board or large area of clean work top
biscuit cutters, 6cm (2½ in) across, star shaped or round
apple corer
baking sheet
clingfilm
red and green ribbon or paper ribbon

Get a grown-up to heat the oven to 350F/180C/gas 4. Put the butter into a bowl. Beat it to make it creamy. Put in the honey and beat it into the butter. In another bowl, mix the flour with the mixed spice. Beat this mixture into the butter and honey, adding only a little of it at a time and making sure that it is well mixed in. Now use your fingers to bring the dough into a smooth ball. Dust it with flour.

Sprinkle more flour onto a work surface. Roll out the dough so it is about 6mm (¼ in) thick. Cut out shapes with your biscuit cutters. Using an apple corer, stamp a hole in the centre of each shape. If you do not have an apple corer you can cut a hole in each one using a blunt knife. Gather up all the spare pieces of dough into a ball. Roll it out again and cut more shapes. Do this until you have used up all the dough.

Sprinkle the biscuit tray with flour. Put on the biscuits and bake them for 20 minutes so they are firm but not coloured. Cool them on the baking sheet for 5 minutes and then lift them onto a wire rack to cool completely.

Wrap each biscuit in clingfilm, snipping it in the centre of the biscuit and wrapping it round the centre edges to make the hole and to keep the biscuit fresh. Tie coloured ribbon or paper ribbon through each biscuit leaving enough to make loops for hanging on the Christmas tree.

# CHRISTMAS PARTY INVITATIONS

Grey Rabbit wrote her party invitations on holly leaves and gave them to Robin the postman to deliver to her friends.
Here is how to make them.

You will need:

a piece of thin white card, 40cm × 11.5cm (16 in × 4½ in)
thick paper 20cm × 11.5cm (8 in × 4½ in)
pencil
scissors
felt-tipped pens

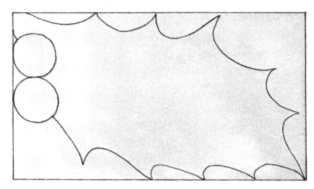

First make your template like this. On the left hand, narrow, side of the piece of paper, draw two large holly berries, close together and coming against the edge. Draw a holly leaf attached to the berries, using up most of the paper. Cut out the shape you have drawn. You can now make a lot of invitations all the same shape by using this template. If you only need to make one or two invitations, you can draw the leaf directly onto the card.

Fold the piece of card in half along the narrow side. Place the paper template on the card with the holly berries against the fold. Draw round it.
Cut out the card through two layers to make a holly leaf which opens.

On the inside, draw a dotted line along the fold and write 'cut' in small letters underneath it.
Using a black felt-tipped pen, outline the shape of the berries. Colour the berries red and the leaf green.
Using a fountain pen with black ink or a black ball-point pen, write the invitation on the front of the holly leaf:

DEAR ...........
PLEASE COME TO MY PARTY
ON...........
AT ...........
MY ADDRESS IS...........
LOVE FROM...........
RSVP

RSVP (This does not mean, as Grey Rabbit thought, 'Rat shan't visit party! It means 'Reply if you please'.)

On the inside half of the card write:

The person to whom you send your invitation can then cut off the back half along the dotted line and send it back to you.

DEAR ...........
THANK YOU, I CAN/CANNOT COME TO YOUR PARTY
LOVE FROM ...........

# CHRISTMAS FOOD and DRINK

When the carol singers visited her house, Grey Rabbit gave them hot mince pies and primrose wine that had been warmed over the fire.

Here is how to make the pies, and also a hot fruity punch that you can offer to your own Christmas visitors.

## MINCE PIES
You will need:

225g (8 oz) flour, plus more for rolling out
$\frac{1}{4}$ teaspoon salt
100g (4 oz) butter
8 tablespoons cold water
12 teaspoons mincemeat
1 egg, beaten
bowl
blunt knife
rolling pin
6cm (2$\frac{1}{2}$ in) biscuit cutter

Get a grown-up to heat the oven to 400F/200C/gas 6.

Put the flour and salt into a mixing bowl. Cut the butter into small pieces. Add it to the flour and rub it in with your fingers so the mixture looks like fine breadcrumbs. Add the water and mix everything to a dough.

Sprinkle flour on a work surface. Roll out the dough. Using your biscuit cutter, stamp out 24 rounds.

Line twelve patty tins with half the rounds. Put a teaspoon of mincemeat into each one. Cover the mincemeat with the other twelve rounds, pressing them down round the edges to seal them.

Brush the tops with the beaten egg. Bake the pies for 15 minutes or until they are golden brown. Serve them hot or put them onto wire racks to cool.

## HOT FRUITY PUNCH
You will need:

1.15 litres (2 pints) red grape juice
1.15 litres (2 pints) orange juice
100g (4 oz) honey
2 cinnamon sticks

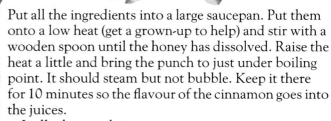

Put all the ingredients into a large saucepan. Put them onto a low heat (get a grown-up to help) and stir with a wooden spoon until the honey has dissolved. Raise the heat a little and bring the punch to just under boiling point. It should steam but not bubble. Keep it there for 10 minutes so the flavour of the cinnamon goes into the juices.

Ladle the punch into mugs.

# CHRISTMAS PARTY GAMES

When Grey Rabbit and her friends had a party, they played jolly party games, like Blind Man's Buff, Turn the Trencher and Hunt the Thimble. Hare's favourite party game was Turn the Trencher. Here is how to play it.

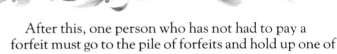

## Turn the Trencher

Everyone must sit round in a large circle. One person must come to the middle of the circle to 'turn the trencher'. The trencher is something large and round that can be spun easily, such as round tin tray or the lid from a round biscuit tin or a round bread board.

The person in the centre spins the 'trencher', calling out the name of one of the people in the circle as he does so. The person called has to run up to catch the trencher before it falls. If he can catch it, he spins the trencher again immediately, calling out the name of someone else. If he lets the trencher fall, then he must pay a forfeit by putting at the side of the room something small belonging to him, such as a handkerchief, a shoe or a scarf. If the person has nothing to give, he must write his name on a piece of paper instead. After this, he turns the trencher and the game should carry on until everyone has had a go at catching it.

After this, one person who has not had to pay a forfeit must go to the pile of forfeits and hold up one of them, saying:

"Here is a thing and a very pretty thing, and what is the owner to do?"

Someone must answer:

"He must cry in one corner, laugh in another, dance in another and sing in another."

The person who owns the forfeit that has been held up must do just that and afterwards, hold up one of the other forfeits for someone else to claim. The game ends when all the forfeits have been claimed.

# Hunt the Thimble

Grey Rabbit enjoyed playing Hunt the Thimble, but if you don't have a thimble you can use something else that is as small and easy to hide.

One person takes the thimble and everyone else goes out of the room. While they are out, the person with the thimble must hide it, but not swallow it like Wise Owl! When he has done so, he calls in the rest who have to find it. The first person to find the thimble hides it the next time. The thimble must be hidden so that people do not have to turn things over to look for it. They should be able to spot it by looking carefully.

# Charades

After Hunt the Thimble, Grey Rabbit and her friends asked each other riddles. Charades are rather like riddles that you have to act.

To play Charades, divide up into groups of two or three people, depending on how many are at the party. One group must go out of the room and, while the others are waiting, choose a word that can be split up into at least two syllables or sections, such as 'pullover' (pull, over). They must then make up three short scenes to act in front of the others. In the first, they must somewhere say the first part of the word, the second part must come into the second scene and the whole word in the third scene. Try not to make the parts and the whole word too obvious in the scenes, to make it harder for the others to guess what your chosen word is.

# Variations

Choose the name of a film or book and act each important word in that name; or act out the meaning of the name without giving the words.

# Oranges and Lemons

Hare would have loved to play Oranges and Lemons. This is how the song goes:

*'Oranges and lemons,' say the bells of St Clements.*
*'You owe me five farthings,' say the bells of St Martins.*
*'When will you pay me?' say the bells of Old Bailey.*
*'When I grow rich,' say the bells of Shoreditch.*
*'When will that be?' say the bells of Stepney.*
*'I do not know,' says the great bell at Bow.*
*Here comes a candle to light you to bed.*
*Here comes a chopper to chop off your head.*
*Chip, chop, chip, chop,*
*The last man's head.*

How to play it:

The two biggest children secretly decide which of them is to be 'oranges' and which of them 'lemons'. They then make an arch. While everybody sings the song the other children go under the arch, going round again when all have gone through. On the last 'head' the arch comes down to trap whoever is underneath it. He is asked whether he wants to be 'oranges' or 'lemons' and has to whisper his answer so that the rest do not hear. When all the children have been caught, there is a tug of war between 'oranges' and 'lemons'.

Little Grey Rabbit ended her party
with a dance and they all danced
the polka, while Hare played his flute.

# CHRISTMAS CAROLS

To go out carol singing with a group of friends is a wonderful way of getting into the Christmas spirit. You must have some grown-ups with you and their voices will swell the sound of the music. Sometimes neighbours will invite you in for a hot drink or a mince pie. And most people will want to give you something for your efforts!

On Christmas Eve, Grey Rabbit, Squirrel and Hare were visited by the Waits, a band of travelling singers who sang Christmas carols at the doors of all the animals in the neighbourhood. Here are some verses of the carols they sang.

## I SAW THREE SHIPS

*I saw three ships come sailing in,*
*On Christmas Day, on Christmas Day,*
*I saw three ships come sailing in,*
*On Christmas Day in the morning.*

*And what was in those ships all three?*
*On Christmas Day etc.*

*Our Saviour Christ and his lady.*
*On Christmas Day etc.*

*Pray, whither sailed those ships all three?*
*On Christmas Day etc.*

*O, they sailed into Bethlehem.*
*On Christmas Day etc.*

*And all the bells on earth shall ring.*
*On Christmas Day etc.*

*And all the Angels in Heaven shall sing.*
*On Christmas Day etc.*

*And all the souls on earth shall sing.*
*On Christmas Day etc.*

*Then let us all rejoice again!*
*On Christmas Day etc.*

## GREEN GROWS THE HOLLY

*Green grows the holly,*
*So doth the ivy;*
*Though winter blasts blow ne'er so high,*
*Green grows the holly.*

*Green grows the holly,*
*So doth the ivy;*
*The God of life can never die,*
*Hope! saith the holly.*

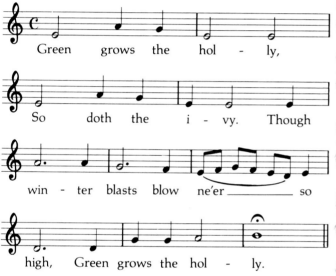

## THE MOON SHINES BRIGHT

*The moon shines bright*
*And the stars give a light:*
*A little before it was day.*
*The Lord, our God, he called on us,*
*And bid us awake and pray.*

This one is Grey Rabbit's favourite carol:

## HOLLY RED AND MISTLETOE WHITE

*Holly red and mistletoe white,*
*The stars are shining with golden light,*
*Burning like candles this Holy Night.*
*Holly red and mistletoe white.*

*Mistletoe white and holly red,*
*The day is over, we're off to bed,*
*Tired body and sleepy head,*
*Mistletoe white and holly red.*